Wild Flowers of

the Dorset Coast Path

Peter & Margaret Cramb

P. & M. Cramb

First published in 2003
by P. & M. Cramb
32 Pitchers, Salway Ash,
Bridport, Dorset DT6 5QS

ISBN 0 9537746 1 9

British Library Cataloguing-in-Publication Data.
A catalogue record for this book is
available from the British Library.

Typeset by Dorchester Typesetting, Bridport Road,
Dorchester, Dorset DT1 1UA

Printed by The Friary Press, Bridport Road,
Dorchester, Dorset DT1 1JL

CONTENTS

Cover photograph: the coast path
near Burton Bradstock

LIST OF PLATES

INTRODUCTION

Every year many thousands of people enjoy the magnificent scenery along the Dorset coast path. If you are among them, you will also see many beautiful wild flowers, but may be able to name only a few of the different species.

Although there are several excellent wild flower guides available, these usually cover a wide area, such as the whole of the British Isles. As a result, identification is often a time-consuming and frustrating process. The aim of this book is to help you to identify the wild flowers you see along the path by including only species which are found there.

We have covered just over 100 species, our intention being to give a good cross-section – but not a complete coverage – of the flowers you will see most often. In deciding which flowers to include, we have given priority to those found only, or mostly, on the coast, although others are included if common along the path. We have also chosen species which we think you will find particularly noticeable, interesting or attractive. Finally, we have selected some rarer flowers, particularly those for which the Dorset coast is an important locality.

We have included only what in everyday language are called flowers and so have excluded other types of flowering plants such as grasses, sedges and rushes.

Each flower species is illustrated and described in the text, which we have tried to keep as short and clear as possible. There are also photographs of some of the flowers, not only to aid identification but also to show their beauty and inspire you to search them out for yourselves!

By the Dorset coast path we mean the part of the South West Coast Path between Lyme Regis in the west and the mouth of Poole Harbour in the east; we also include the path round the coast of Portland. For much of its way the path runs through the Dorset and East Devon Coast World Heritage Site. This was designated in 2001 in recognition of the exceptional geological importance of the coast; the splendour and diversity of its geology are well reflected in the beauty and variety of its wild flowers.

We hope that this book will increase your enjoyment of the flowers of the coast path, and stimulate a desire to conserve them for the benefit of future generations.

HOW THE BOOK IS ARRANGED

Habitats

We have grouped the flowers into the type of natural surroundings, or *habitat* (for example, dry grassland, shingle or sandy places), in which they are typically found along the coast path. At the beginning of each group we have briefly described the main features of the habitat and given some examples of where it may be found along the path: the National Trail Guide 'South West Coast Path, Exmouth to Poole' (see bibliography) will enable you to locate these places.

The inclusion of a flower in a particular habitat should not be seen as hard and fast, as some species, especially the common ones, are tolerant of a wide variety of different conditions and can be found in several different types of habitat. It is also sometimes difficult to identify habitats clearly as they frequently overlap or have indistinct boundaries; for example, in areas of sand mixed with shingle, or dry grassland on a cliff top. In these situations we suggest you look for the flower under both of the habitats concerned. Further information on the location of species can be found in 'The Flora of Dorset' (see bibliography).

Flowering Periods

Within each habitat the flowers are placed in order of their flowering periods. For example, in the hedgerows and verges habitat Lords-and-Ladies, with a flowering period of April to May, is shown before Hedge Bedstraw, with a flowering period of June to September.

Flowering periods can vary a great deal due to factors such as the aspect of the site where the plant is growing or weather differences from season to season. Nevertheless, the periods shown, which are based mainly on our own experience, show when you are most likely to see each species in flower along the path.

The Illustrations

The illustrations are intended to depict the plants as they look naturally, showing the general appearance of the flowers and leaves, but not necessarily all the botanical details. For some species there are additional illustrations of the flowers, either at a larger scale where they are small in relation to the rest of the plant, or showing them from a different angle. The plants are not all drawn to the same scale and you will find guidance about their size by referring to the height of the plant and the flower measurement shown in the descriptions.

The Descriptions

The first lines of the description give the *English name*, followed by the *scientific name*: in both cases we have followed the names used in Stace's 'New Flora of the British Isles' (see bibliography). For a few species we have also shown an alternative English name, if commonly used.

We then show the *flowering period*, *flower colour* and *height* of a typical specimen of the plant – short: under 20cm; medium: 20-50cm; tall: over 50cm. Where split heights, e.g. short/medium, are shown, the height can fall into either range.

If applicable, we then give the *main* – but not necessarily all – additional habitats in which the plant is found along the path, together with further information such as its more specific habitat requirements and habit of growth.

The remainder of the description gives brief details of the flowers – size refers to the diameter of a typical specimen unless otherwise stated – and leaves. The fruit – the part containing the seeds – and stems are also described if they are useful aids to identification.

Our aim has been to keep the descriptions as short as possible by including only information which, taken together with the illustrations, is needed to enable the plant to be identified. Where species can be confused with others, including some not described elsewhere in this book, we have set out the main differences which enable them to be distinguished. Further details of the species covered, together with descriptions of others you may see along the path, may be found in books such as Collins Pocket Guide 'The Wild Flowers of Britain and Northern Europe' and 'The Wild Flower Key' (see bibliography).

Where a flower is shown as scarce or rare this refers to its occurrence *along the path*, unless otherwise stated; 'nationally scarce' refers to its occurrence in Britain as indicated by the 'New Atlas of the British & Irish Flora' (see bibliography).

All the flowers described in the book are considered to be native to Britain, except those shown as 'introduced'; these have been brought in by humans, for example, as garden plants, and become naturalised in the wild.

Technical Terms

We have avoided using technical terms as far as possible. Flower parts mentioned in the descriptions are shown in the drawing below.

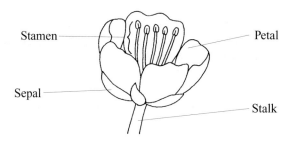

The following sections headed 'Labiate Family', 'Composite Flowers' and 'Soils' explain a few further technical terms used.

Labiate Family

This family includes flowers such as Betony, Ground-ivy and Wild Marjoram which have certain characteristics in common. The flowers usually have a petal-tube with 2 lips, an upper and a lower, separated so that the mouth is open. The leaves are usually in opposite pairs and the stems square. The flowers and leaves are frequently aromatic, particularly when crushed.

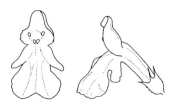

Betony, a typical labiate flower

Composite Flowers

This very large family includes such different flowers as daisies, thistles and dandelions. What they have in common is that each flower head consists of many individual tiny flowers, or *florets*.

Each floret has petals joined in a tube. Sometimes the tube ends in 5 small teeth to give a *disc* floret. At other times the tube is split and one side extended to give a petal-like *ray* floret.

There are 3 types of composite flowers:
1) Those with disc florets in the centre and ray florets outside, such as daisies.
2) Those with disc, but no ray, florets, such as thistles.
3) Those with ray, but no disc, florets, such as dandelions.

Underneath the flower head is a ring of *bracts*, resembling sepals.

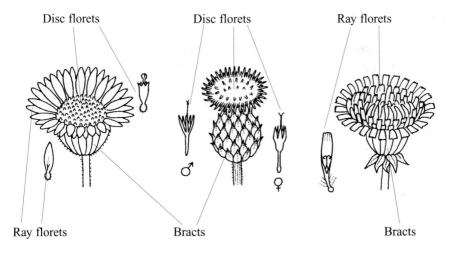

Disc florets   Disc florets   Ray florets

♂   ♀

Ray florets   Bracts   Bracts

DISC & RAY FLORETS   DISC FLORETS ONLY   RAY FLORETS ONLY
e.g. daisies   e.g. thistles   e.g. dandelions

Soils

Soil types are very important in influencing where different species of flowers can be found. In particular, the level of acidity or otherwise of a soil will determine which species are able to grow in it.

We can divide soils into 3 groups depending on their acidity: *acid, neutral* and *calcareous* (alkaline). Some flowers are quite specific in their requirements and will only grow, for example, in calcareous soils. Others are less demanding and will grow happily in a range of soils from acid to calcareous. Generally speaking, acid soils support a narrower range of flowers than either neutral or calcareous soils.

The soil in an area very often reflects its underlying geology. Much of the path runs through areas of chalk or limestone which give rise to highly calcareous soils, leading in turn to a rich variety of beautiful flowers.

Useful Tips

- Many flowers grow in more than one habitat and so be prepared to look in various sections for the one you are trying to identify.
- There can be considerable variation between individual plants of the same species in size, shape and flower colour. Be prepared to make allowance for this.
- While not essential for the identification of the flowers in this book, a *hand lens* will add greatly to your enjoyment of them by revealing much beautiful detail. A magnification of about 10 times is recommended.

Please do not pick wild flowers – leave them for others to enjoy.

Safety Warning

Several stretches of the path run along cliff tops and some of these are subject to landslips.

In the interests of safety, please therefore **always**:
- keep strictly to the marked path.
- observe any indicated diversions.
- keep well back from cliff edges.
- take special care in poor weather conditions.

Please also strictly observe all instructions on the Lulworth army ranges and the rifle range at Chickerell.

HEDGEROWS AND VERGES

Hedgerows are field boundaries formed from bushes and trees, sometimes on a grassy bank or with a ditch at the side. Verges are narrow strips of grass beside roads or tracks; they often merge into the hedgerows. We have also included in this habitat scrub – low-growing, often stunted, bushes and trees, often in rough or exposed places.

Most of the flowers found in these places also grow in other habitats. When shade and shelter are provided by bushes and trees, flowers are found which may also occur in woodland; in more open areas, the flowers tend to be those which are also found in grassland.

As with other habitats, soil type has an important effect on the number and type of different flower species found (see 'Soils', page 14). Naturalness is also important; for example, a long-established, unaltered verge will support a far greater variety of species than one recently sown or treated with weedkiller.

Where found on the path

This habitat is found in many places on the path, but good examples are found between Burton Bradstock and Abbotsbury and around Ringstead.

Alexanders
(Smyrnium olusatrum)
Mar – Jun   Yellow   Tall
Other habitat: cliffs.
Often in large clumps.
FLOWERS: 5mm; in umbrella-shaped
clusters; 5 well-separated petals,
curled over towards centre;
prominent stamens. Strong smell.
LEAVES: shiny; repeatedly dividing 3
ways into toothed leaflets; base
sheathing stem. Aromatic when
crushed.
Introduced in Roman times.

Ground-ivy
(Glechoma hederacea)
Mar – Jun   Bluish violet   Short
Other habitat: dry grassland.
Creeping with rooting runners;
patch-forming.
FLOWERS: 1cm long; labiate, lower lip
3-lobed, centre lobe purple-spotted.
Aromatic.
LEAVES: often reddish-tinged when
young, turning greener; hairy;
toothed; stalked. Strongly and
distinctively aromatic when crushed.

Lords-and-Ladies, Cuckoo-pint
(Arum maculatum)
Apr – May   Light green (sheath)
Medium
FLOWERS: tiny, not visible; below a
purplish "finger" inside a partly
unfolded fleshy sheath.
Strong smell.
FRUIT: scarlet berries in a short
cylinder.
LEAVES: sometimes dark-spotted;
slightly shiny; fleshy; triangular
with winged bases, wavy-edged;
on long stalks, mostly from base.
Unusual and very distinctive.

Hoary Cress
(Lepidium draba)
Apr – Aug   White   Medium/Tall
Other habitats: shingle, cliffs.
Often in large clumps.
FLOWERS: 7mm; in umbrella-
shaped clusters; 4 well-separated
petals, in cross shape; prominent
yellowish-tipped stamens. Cressy
smell.
LEAVES: light green; softly hairy;
narrow, pointed, often wavy-
edged, slightly toothed; unstalked,
clasping stem.
STEMS: rather spindly.
Introduced in the early 19th
century.

Stinking Iris, Gladdon
(Iris foetidissima)
May – Jul   Purple and
yellowish   Medium/Tall
Other habitats: dry grassland,
cliffs.
FLOWERS: 7cm across; in
spikes; 3 large and 3 smaller
petal-like parts.
FRUIT: capsules splitting into 3
parts holding orange seeds.
LEAVES: darkish green; slightly
shiny; blade-like with
lengthways ridges; mostly
growing from base. Strong
smell when crushed.
Adds a garden feel to the path!
See photograph plate 1.

Creeping Cinquefoil
(Potentilla reptans)
May – Sep   Yellow   Short
Other habitats: dry grassland,
shingle.
Often in bare places.
Creeping with long red rooting
stems; often in large carpeting
patches.
FLOWERS: 2cm; alone on long
hairy stalks; 5 well-separated,
heart-shaped petals; prominent
yellow stamens.
LEAVES: hairy; each with 5 – 7
toothed leaflets; on long hairy
stalks.

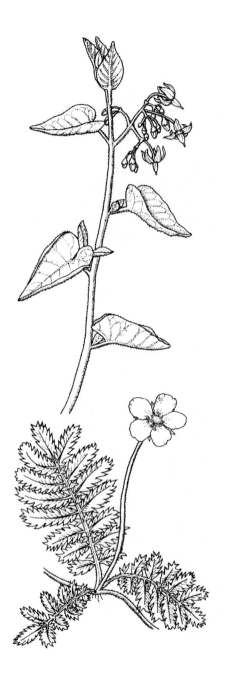

Bittersweet, Woody Nightshade
(Solanum dulcamara)
May – Sep   Violet purple   Medium/
Tall
Other habitat: shingle.
Variable in habit: usually scrambling
but low-growing on shingle.
FLOWERS: 1.5cm; in drooping clusters;
5 turned-back petals, joined at base;
yellow centre.
FRUIT: red berries.
LEAVES: light green, prominently
veined; usually softly hairy; pointed
oval, sometimes nearly arrow-shaped;
edges often turned inwards; stalked.
STEMS: woody at base.

Silverweed
(Potentilla anserina)
May – Sep   Yellow   Short
Often in wet places.
Other habitat: shingle.
Creeping with long reddish rooting
runners.
FLOWERS: 2.5cm; alone on long, hairy
stalks; 5 wavy-edged petals; prominent
yellow stamens.
LEAVES: silvery green, especially below;
silkily hairy; each with about 6 – 10
pairs of toothed leaflets and a single
leaflet at the end.

Tree-mallow
(Lavatera arborea)
May – Oct   Pinkish purple   Tall
Other habitats: waste ground,
shingle, cliffs.
FLOWERS: 4cm; 5 overlapping,
wavy-edged petals, pinkish purple
with darker veins and bases;
prominent mass of white-tipped
stamens.
LEAVES: light green; softly hairy;
wavy-edged, wrinkled; shallow,
toothed lobes; long-stalked.
STEMS: upper reddish; lower brown,
woody.
Native, but also found as a garden
escape.
See **Common Mallow** (page 70).

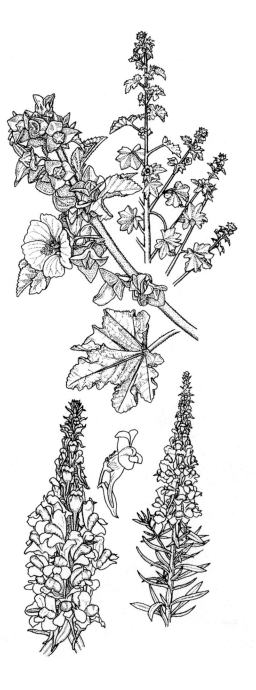

Common Toadflax
(Linaria vulgaris)
May – Oct   Yellow and orange
Medium/Tall
Other habitats: dry grassland,
shingle, cliffs.
FLOWERS: 1.5cm across; in dense
spikes; 2-lipped, closed-mouthed;
pale yellow with orange centre;
lower lip 3-lobed; long pointed
spur beneath.
LEAVES: greyish green; central vein
with prominent rib below; very
narrow with pointed tip; unstalked.
Closely related to the Antirrhinum.

Wild Madder
(Rubia peregrina)
Jun – Aug   Greenish yellow   Medium/Tall
Often in scrub.
Other habitats: dry grassland, rocks, cliffs.
Scrambles over surrounding vegetation or
rocks.
FLOWERS: 8mm; in clusters; usually 5 pointed
petals, joined at base.
FRUIT: black berries.
LEAVES: often dark green; fairly shiny;
prominent central vein; leathery; pointed tip,
prickly edges and rib below; in whorls of
about 4 – 5 around stem.
STEMS: prickly.

Hedge Bedstraw
(Galium mollugo)
Jun – Sep   White or creamy   Medium/Tall
Other habitats: dry grassland, rocks, cliffs.
Often scrambles over surrounding
vegetation.
Variable.
FLOWERS: 4mm; in sometimes dense clusters;
4 pointed petals, in cross shape, joined at
base.
LEAVES: darkish green; shiny; narrow with
pointed tip; in whorls of about 6 – 8 around
stem.
STEMS: smooth.

Cleavers *(Galium aparine)* is similar but
sticky-feeling due to hooked bristles on
stems and leaves.

Great Willowherb
(Epilobium hirsutum)
Jun – Sep   Purplish pink   Tall
Usually in damp places.
Often in large clumps.
FLOWERS: 2.5cm; on hairy, reddish
stalks; 4 overlapping, heart-shaped,
wavy-edged petals with whitish
veins and bases.
FRUIT: long, narrow capsules.
LEAVES: attractively veined; softly
hairy; narrow, pointed, saw-
toothed; unstalked, partly clasping
stem.
Can grow up to 2m tall.

Tufted Vetch
(Vicia cracca)
Jun – Sep   Bluish purple
Medium/Tall
Other habitat: dry grassland.
Clambers over surrounding
vegetation.
FLOWERS: 1cm long; pea-type; in
long-stalked, one-sided spikes;
bluish purple with darker veins.
LEAVES: greyish green below; hairy;
each with about 6 – 10 pairs of
narrow leaflets and a usually
branched tendril at the end; pointed
tip to each leaflet.

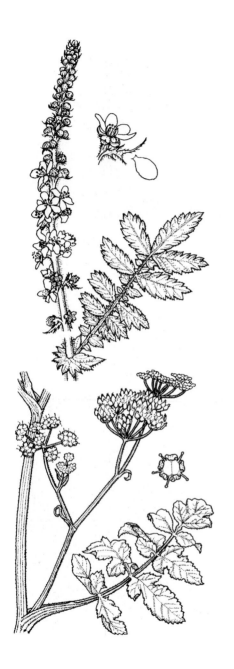

Agrimony
(Agrimonia eupatoria)
Jun – Sep   Yellow   Medium/Tall
Other habitat: dry grassland.
FLOWERS: 1cm; in long spikes; 5
petals; many golden yellow
stamens.
LEAVES: each with about 4 pairs of
hairy, deeply-toothed leaflets;
smaller leaflets between main ones
and a single leaflet at the end.
STEMS: very hairy.

Wild Parsnip
(Pastinaca sativa var. *sativa)*
Jun – Oct   Yellow   Short/
Medium/Tall
Usually on calcareous soils.
Other habitats: dry grassland,
shingle.
FLOWERS: 4mm; in umbrella-shaped
clusters; 5 petals, curled over
towards centre; prominent yellow
stamens.
LEAVES: hairy; divided into wavy-
edged leaflets with toothed lobes;
base sheathing stem.
STEMS: hairy, deeply furrowed.
Closely related to the cultivated
parsnip.

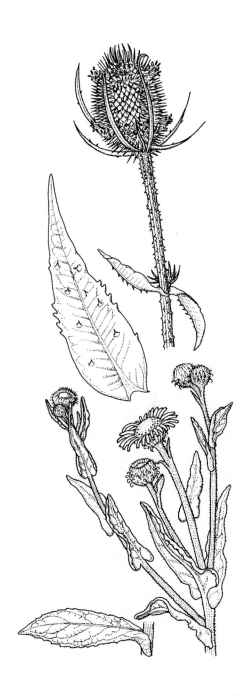

Wild Teasel
(Dipsacus fullonum)
Jul – Oct   Pale purple   Tall
Other habitats: waste ground,
cliffs.
FLOWERS: 5cm (head); egg-shaped;
composite-like; prominent
stamens; softly spiny. Pleasant
sweet smell.
LEAVES: often pimply above;
prickly rib below; upper narrow,
pointed, lower broader; unstalked,
in opposite pairs often joined in a
cup shape around stem.
STEMS: prickly.
The dead flower heads remain
over the winter.

Common Fleabane
(Pulicaria dysenterica)
Jul – Oct   Golden yellow
Medium/Tall
Often in damp places.
Other habitat: shingle.
Frequently in large clumps.
FLOWERS: 2.5cm; composite with
disc florets and short ray florets.
Smell of cats!
LEAVES: light green; attractively
veined; softly hairy; narrow,
pointed, wavy-edged, slightly
toothed; unstalked, clasping stem.
STEMS: woolly-haired.

DRY GRASSLAND AND WASTE GROUND

As with hedgerows and verges, the number of different flower species found in grassland depends considerably on its naturalness.

Most grassland has been substantially changed by agricultural operations such as ploughing, and the use of fertilisers and pesticides. This has resulted in a large reduction in the number of flower species present. The greatest variety is therefore found in areas too small or inaccessible to be intensively farmed, for example, on steep slopes or near cliff tops, or which have become nature reserves. Regular cutting or moderate grazing by livestock is, however, usually beneficial by protecting species which would otherwise be crowded out by stronger-growing plants.

Soil type is also very important in influencing the species found in grassland. We have shown separately those which usually have a preference for calcareous soils and those which tend to be equally at home in other types of soil found along the path (see 'Soils' page 14).

"Waste ground" includes a variety of places such as field edges, disturbed ground, car parks and the sites of old buildings which start to revert to nature and become colonised by grassland species.

Where found on the path

Excellent examples of calcareous dry grassland are found in areas of chalk or limestone, such as between White Nothe and Lulworth Cove, and in many parts of Purbeck.

Other dry grassland is found scattered along the path, for example, in the section between Charmouth and West Bay.

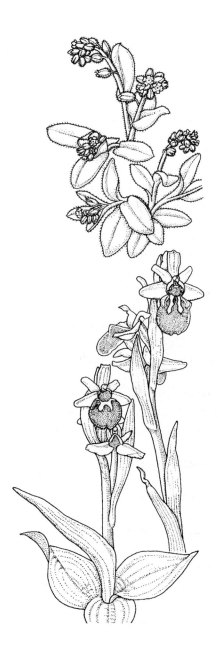

Early Forget-me-not
(Myosotis ramosissima)
Apr – May   Bright blue   Short
Other habitats: sandy places, cliffs.
In bare places or short turf.
FLOWERS: 2mm; in curled spikes; 5
petals, joined at base, with white
bases and yellow centre.
LEAVES: Light green, often reddish-
tinged; very hairy.
Often tiny and easily overlooked but a
joy to find.

Early Spider-orchid
(Ophrys sphegodes)
Apr – May   Brown & yellow   Short
In short turf.
FLOWERS: 2cm; in short spike; lip – the
body of the spider – velvety, reddish
brown with shiny violet π mark;
greenish yellow parts above.
LEAVES: upper narrow, pointed,
clasping or sheathing stem; lower
broader, in rosette at base.
Nationally scarce; its only Dorset
sites are in Purbeck. The logo of the
Dorset Wildlife Trust.
See photograph plate 2.

Horseshoe Vetch
(Hippocrepis comosa)
Apr – Jul Yellow Short/Medium
Other habitat: cliffs.
Sometimes cushion-forming.
FLOWERS: 1cm long; pea-type; in
long-stalked heads; petals yellow
with reddish brown veins. Strong
sweet smell.
LEAVES: each with about 4 – 5 well-
separated pairs of leaflets and a
single leaflet at the end; pointed tip
to each leaflet.
The foodplant for caterpillars of the
beautiful Adonis Blue butterfly.

Common Milkwort
(Polygala vulgaris)
Apr – Oct   Blue, pink or white
Short
Often weak and straggly.
FLOWERS: 8mm long; in spikes; 3
joined petals with 2 large petal-like
sepals and 3 small other sepals.
LEAVES: upper narrow, pointed,
lower shorter, broader; arranged
alternately along the stem.

Chalk Milkwort *(Polygala
calcarea)* is similar but has flowers
usually very bright blue and upper
leaves blunter. Not usually in
flower after June. Scarce.

Oxeye Daisy
(Leucanthemum vulgare)
Apr – Oct   White   Medium/Tall
Other habitats: verges, cliffs.
FLOWERS: 4cm; composite with yellow
disc florets and white ray florets – like
large daisies.
LEAVES: often dark green; toothed or
lobed; upper narrow, clasping stem,
lower spoon-shaped.

Sea and **Scentless Mayweeds** (page
56) have similar flowers but leaves
deeply divided into segments.

Early Gentian
(Gentianella anglica)
May – Jun   Mauvish purple   Short
In short turf.
FLOWERS: 1cm across; bell-shaped with
4 or 5 pointed petal lobes. Usually
only open in bright light.
LEAVES: narrow, pointed; in opposite
pairs.
Sometimes under 5cm tall – an
exquisite flower.
Nationally scarce, but with a good
population in Dorset.
Found only in Britain.
See photograph plate 2.

Autumn Gentian *(Gentianella
amarella)* is similar but usually
flowers in August – September.

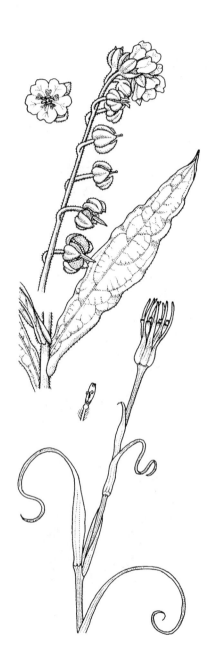

Hound's-tongue
(Cynoglossum officinale)
May – Jul   Maroon turning blue
Medium/Tall
Other habitat: shingle.
Noticeably upright.
FLOWERS: 8mm; in one-sided spikes;
usually drooping; 5 joined petals,
attractively veined; maroon turning to
purplish deep blue.
FRUIT: bristly nutlets, 4 from each
flower.
LEAVES: light greyish green; softly hairy;
narrow, pointed, wavy-edged; upper
unstalked, lower stalked.
STEMS: very hairy.
Smells of mice!

Goat's-beard
(Tragopogon pratensis ssp. *minor)*
May – Sep   Yellow   Medium/Tall
Usually in long grass.
FLOWERS: 2.5cm; alone on long stalks;
composite with ray florets only; bracts
much longer than rays. Usually only
fully open on sunny mornings. Pleasant
sweet smell.
FRUIT: held in large dandelion-like
"clocks".
LEAVES: very narrow, pointed, grass-like;
often curling at tip.
STEMS: milky-juiced.

Salad Burnet
(Sanguisorba minor ssp. *minor)*
May – Sep   Green and red
Short/Medium
FLOWERS: 3mm (female), 5mm
(male); in long-stalked spherical
heads; no petals, 4 greenish
sepals; upper flowers of head
female with protruding red brush-
like parts; lower flowers male with
many long drooping reddish- or
yellowish-tipped stamens.
LEAVES: each with about 6 – 10
pairs of toothed leaflets and a
single leaflet at the end.

Kidney Vetch
(Anthyllis vulneraria)
May – Oct   Yellow   Short/
Medium
Other habitats: shingle, cliffs.
Variable.
FLOWERS: 1.5cm long; pea-type; in
long-stalked, very hairy heads,
usually in pairs or threes.
LEAVES: greyish green; silkily
hairy, especially below; each with
about 3 – 5 pairs of leaflets and a
single, often larger, leaflet at the
end; pointed tip to each leaflet.
The foodplant for caterpillars of
the tiny Small Blue butterfly.

Common Broomrape
(Orobanche minor)
Jun – Jul   Purplish yellow   Short/
Medium
Other habitat: cliffs.
Variable.
FLOWERS: 1.5cm long; in spike; 2-
lipped; yellow tinged purplish;
purple lobes inside.
LEAVES: none, replaced by small
pointed brownish scales.
A parasite on the roots of other
plants, usually of the pea family or
Sea Carrot (page 71).

Ivy Broomrape *(Orobanche
hederae)* is similar but has flowers
with yellow lobes inside. Found on
ivy, often in old quarries; scarce.
See photograph plate 14.

Bee Orchid
(Ophrys apifera)
Jun – Jul   Brown, yellowish and
pink   Short/Medium
Other habitat: cliffs.
FLOWERS: 2.5cm; in spike; lip – the
back of the bee – velvety, dark brown
with yellowish markings; pink parts
behind.
LEAVES: light green; narrow, pointed;
upper clasping or sheathing stem,
lower in rosette at base.
Most attractive, although often
elusive.
See photograph plate 3.

Pyramidal Orchid
(Anacamptis pyramidalis)
Jun – Aug   Purplish pink   Short/
Medium
Other habitat: cliffs.
FLOWERS: 7mm; in pyramidal spike
becoming longer and more cylindrical
with age; lip 3-lobed, long narrow spur
behind. Sometimes smells of foxes.
LEAVES: light green; narrow, pointed;
upper clasping or sheathing stem, lower
in rosette at base.
Very striking, sometimes in
breathtaking groups!
See photographs plates 4 & 5.

Betony
(Stachys officinalis)
Jun – Sep   Bright purple   Short/
Medium
FLOWERS: 1.5cm long; in hemispherical
or more elongated head; labiate, lower
lip 3-lobed; hairy. Aromatic when
crushed.
LEAVES: very hairy; regularly and
attractively toothed; sparse, short-
stalked, on stem, long-stalked at base.
Aromatic when crushed.

Wild Marjoram
(Origanum vulgare)
Jun – Sep   Lilac   Short/Medium
Other habitat: scrub.
FLOWERS: 8mm long; in dense
clusters; labiate, lower lip 3-
lobed; prominent stamens.
Pleasantly and distinctively
aromatic when crushed.
LEAVES: light green; attractively
veined; hairy; pointed oval;
stalked. Pleasantly aromatic when
crushed.
Grown as the culinary herb
oregano.
A favourite source of nectar for
the Lulworth Skipper butterfly.

Squinancywort
(Asperula cynanchica)
Jun – Sep   Pale pink to white
Short
In bare places or short turf.
Very slender.
FLOWERS: 5mm; in clusters; 4
pointed petals, in cross shape,
joined at base. Usually whitish
with pale pink veins and backs,
but variable.
LEAVES: slightly shiny; narrow
with pointed tip; in often unequal
whorls of usually 4 around stem.
Often tiny and overlooked.

Lady's Bedstraw
(Galium verum)
Jun – Oct   Yellow   Short/
Medium
Other habitats: sandy places,
cliffs.
Straggly, often supporting itself
on surrounding vegetation.
FLOWERS: 4mm; in dense clusters,
sometimes covering the upper
stem; 4 pointed petals, in cross
shape, joined at base. Acrid smell.
LEAVES: dark green; shiny; very
narrow with pointed tip and
curled down edges; in whorls of
about 6-9 around stem.

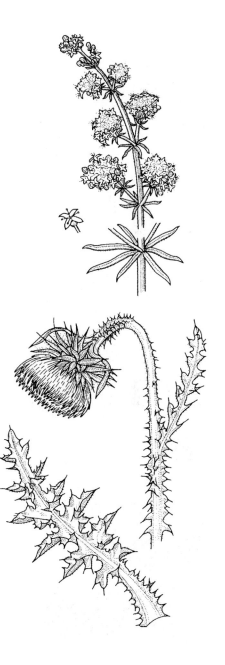

Musk Thistle, Nodding Thistle
(Carduus nutans)
Jun – Oct   Purple   Medium/Tall
Other habitat: cliffs.
FLOWERS: 4cm; often drooping and
nodding in the breeze; composite
with disc florets only; bracts
purplish, hairy, tipped with sharp
yellowish spines. Pleasant sweet
smell.
LEAVES: hairy; narrow, pointed,
wavy-edged; deeply lobed, sharp
yellowish spines on tips.
See photograph plate 2.

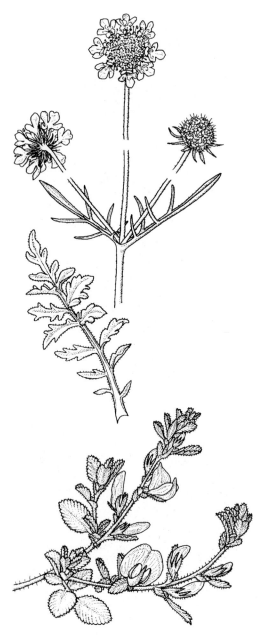

Small Scabious
(Scabiosa columbaria)
Jun – Oct   Mauvish blue   Short/ Medium
Other habitat: cliffs.
FLOWERS: 3cm (head); composite-like; black bristles inside; prominent purplish-tipped stamens; one row of bracts. Pleasant sweet smell.
LEAVES: hairy; upper deeply divided into very narrow lobes, lower with broader lobes or unlobed and toothed.

Field Scabious *(Knautia arvensis)*, often found on verges, is similar but usually larger; its flowerheads are without black bristles inside and have two rows of bracts.

Common Restharrow
(Ononis repens)
Jun – Oct   Pink and white
Short/Medium
Other habitats: shingle, sandy places, cliffs.
Sometimes creeping.
FLOWERS: 1.5cm long; pea-type; in small leafy spikes; pink and white with dark pink veins. Pleasant sweet smell.
LEAVES: stickily hairy; oval, neatly toothed; undivided or with 3 leaflets. Strong smell.
STEMS: reddish, hairy, slightly woody.

Greater Knapweed
(Centaurea scabiosa)
Jun – Oct   Purple   Medium/
Tall
Often in long grass.
Other habitat: cliffs.
FLOWERS: 6cm; composite with
disc florets only but almost
always with ray-like outer
florets; bracts green with dark
brown edges.
LEAVES: roughly hairy; narrow,
pointed; deeply lobed.

Common Knapweed (page 45)
is similar but has flowers only
sometimes with "rays" and
leaves not deeply lobed.

Dwarf Thistle,
Stemless Thistle
(Cirsium acaule)
Jun – Oct   Purple   Short
Often in short turf.
Other habitat: cliffs.
FLOWERS: 4cm; usually nestling
in rosette of leaves on ground,
occasionally on a stem;
composite with disc florets only.
LEAVES: darkish green; hairy
below; narrow, pointed, wavy-
edged; deeply lobed, sharp
yellow spines on tips.
Often found when you sit down
for a picnic!
See photograph plate 3.

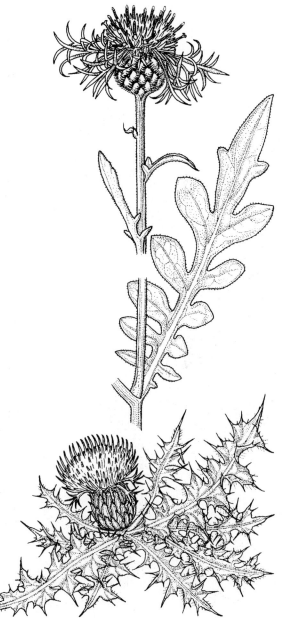

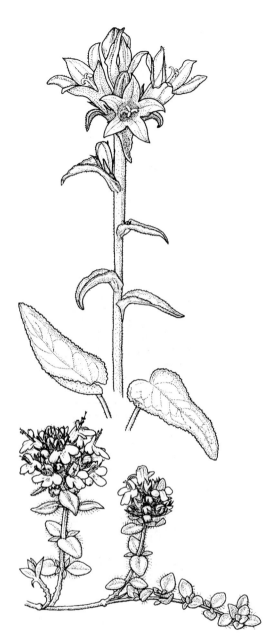

Clustered Bellflower
(Campanula glomerata)
Jun – Oct   Violet   Short/
Medium
FLOWERS: 2cm across; in a tight
cluster at top of stem,
sometimes also lower down;
bell-shaped; usually 5 pointed
petal lobes; violet with darker
veins.
LEAVES: attractively veined;
hairy; pointed, edges turned
inwards; upper narrow,
unstalked, clasping stem; lower
broader, toothed, long-stalked,
growing from base.
Most attractive and striking;
scarce.
See photograph plate 3.

Wild Thyme
(Thymus polytrichus)
Jun – Oct   Pale purple   Short
In short turf; sometimes on ant
hills.
Other habitats: rocks, cliffs.
Mat-forming.
FLOWERS: 8mm long; in
roundish heads; labiate, lower
lip 3-lobed; prominent stamens.
Aromatic when crushed.
LEAVES: shiny; very hairy; oval;
short-stalked. Distinctively
aromatic when crushed.
Closely related to the culinary
herb.

Yellow-wort
(Blackstonia perfoliata)
Jun – Oct   Bright yellow   Short/
Medium
Other habitat: cliffs.
FLOWERS: 2cm; usually 8 petals,
overlapping, joined at base. Often
only fully open in sunshine.
LEAVES: pale bluish green; broad;
upper with pointed tips, in opposite
pairs, joined in a cup shape around
stem; lower in rosette at base.

Ploughman's-spikenard
(Inula conyzae)
Jul – Sep   Yellow   Short/
Medium/Tall
Other habitat: cliffs.
Stiffly erect.
FLOWERS: 1cm; in tight clusters;
composite with disc and ray
florets; rays very short, often
obscured by bracts, or missing;
bracts green and purplish.
Pleasantly aromatic.
LEAVES: strongly veined; hairy;
wavy-edged, slightly toothed;
upper unstalked, lower stalked.
STEMS: dark purplish, very hairy.

Carline Thistle
(Carlina vulgaris)
Jul – Oct   Yellow and brown
Short/Medium
Other habitat: cliffs.
FLOWERS: 4cm; composite with
yellowish brown disc florets only;
outer bracts hairy, green to dark
purplish, with sharp yellowish-
tipped spines; inner bracts pale
yellow, ray-like, often closed in
dull or wet weather.
LEAVES: light green; cottony-
haired, especially below; narrow,
pointed, wavy-edged; spiny-lobed.
The dead flower heads remain
over the winter.
See photograph plate 6.

Saw-wort
(Serratula tinctoria)
Jul – Oct   Purple   Short/Medium
Like a spineless thistle.
FLOWERS: 2.5cm; female and male
on separate plants; composite with
disc florets only; bracts purplish,
pointed, neatly arranged. Pleasant
sweet smell.
LEAVES: purplish edges; narrow,
pointed; usually deeply divided
into lobes with fine, saw-like
teeth, sometimes less deeply lobed
or unlobed.
Delicate and graceful. Sometimes
seen in great numbers by the path.

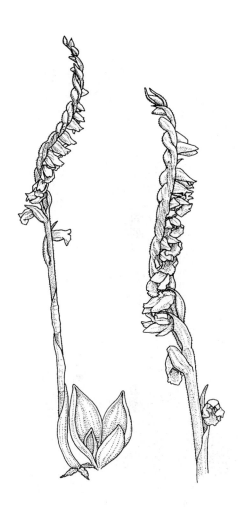

Autumn Lady's-tresses
(Spiranthes spiralis)
Aug – Sep   White   Short
Usually in short turf.
FLOWERS: 5mm long; in a
spiralling spike; tubular; green-
centred. Very pleasant sweet
smell.
LEAVES: upper greyish green,
narrow, pointed, scale-like,
sheathing stem; lower darker,
broader, in rosette at base offset
from stem.
A delightful small orchid; easy to
overlook.
See photograph plate 6.

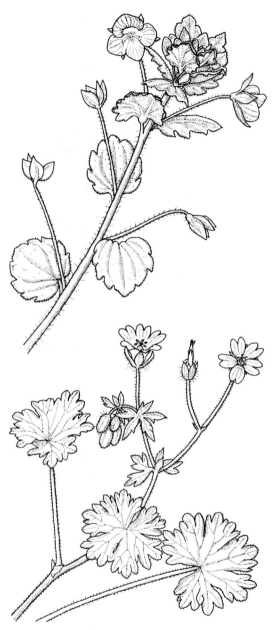

Common Field-speedwell
(Veronica persica)
Jan – Dec   Bright blue and
whitish Short
Often in cultivated or on waste
ground. Sprawling.
FLOWERS: 1cm; alone on long
hairy stalks; 4 petals, joined at
base, bright blue with darker
veins and whitish bases, the
lowest petal usually palest.
LEAVES: light green; hairy;
toothed; short-stalked.
One of several Speedwells
found along the path;
introduced.

Dove's-foot Crane's-bill
(Geranium molle)
Mar – Sep   Pinkish purple
Short/Medium
Other habitats: sandy places,
cliffs. Variable.
FLOWERS: 1cm; 5 heart-shaped
petals. Sometimes very pale.
FRUIT: with narrow, pointed
"crane's bill".
LEAVES: softly hairy; roundish,
cut about half-way to the base
into toothed lobes.

Cut-leaved Crane's-bill
(Geranium dissectum) is
similar but has leaves cut
almost to the base; introduced.
Other species of Crane's-bill
are found, less frequently,
along the path.

**Common Bird's-foot-trefoil,
Eggs-and-Bacon**
(Lotus corniculatus)
Apr – Oct   Bright yellow
Short
Other habitats: shingle, cliffs.
Variable.
FLOWERS: 1.5cm long; pea-type;
usually in long-stalked heads,
sometimes alone; bright yellow
with reddish veins and buds.
Sweetish smell.
LEAVES: often hairy; each with 5
oval leaflets, upper 3 in clover
shape, lower 2 nearly clasping
stem.
Widely found along the path.

Grass Vetchling
(Lathyrus nissolia)
May – Jul   Crimson   Short/
Medium/Tall
Other habitat: hedgerows.
Usually in long grass.
FLOWERS: 1.5cm long; pea-type;
alone or in pairs on long thin
stalks; petals crimson with
darker veins.
LEAVES: very narrow, pointed,
grass-like.
Often hidden in the grass until
you see its vivid flowers.

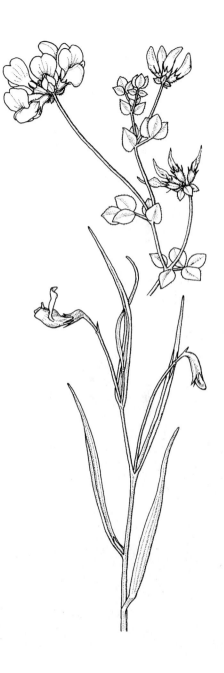

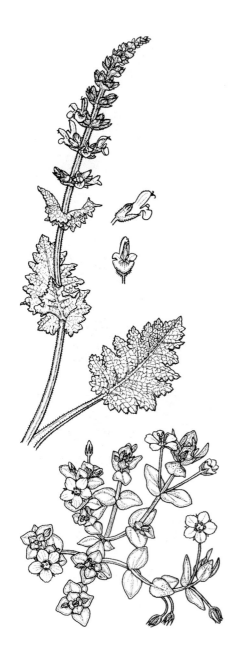

Wild Clary
(Salvia verbenaca)
May – Oct   Bluish violet
Medium/Tall
Other habitats: sandy places, cliffs.
FLOWERS: 1cm long; in gracefully
arching whorled spikes; labiate,
lower lip 3-lobed, whitish throat.
LEAVES: purplish-veined; slightly
hairy; wavy-edged, wrinkled;
toothed lobes; upper unstalked,
clasping stem, lower stalked.
STEMS: purplish, hairy; pleasantly
aromatic when rubbed.

Scarlet Pimpernel
(Anagallis arvensis ssp. *arvensis)*
May – Oct   Pale scarlet   Short
Often in cultivated or on waste
ground.
Other habitats: shingle, sandy
places.
Creeping.
FLOWERS: 1cm; alone on long,
slender stalks; 5 petals, joined at
base, pale scarlet with purple bases;
prominent yellow-tipped stamens.
Usually only open in bright light.
LEAVES: light green; pointed oval;
in opposite pairs; unstalked.

Tall Melilot
(Melilotus altissimus)
Jun – Sep   Yellow   Tall
Other habitat: verges.
FLOWERS: 8mm long; pea-type; in
long-stalked spikes; yellow with
brownish veins at centre.
FRUIT: hairy pods, black when ripe.
LEAVES: greyish green and slightly
hairy below; each with 3 narrow,
saw-toothed leaflets.
Introduced.

Common Knapweed, Hardheads
(Centaurea nigra)
Jun – Nov   Purple   Short/Medium/
Tall
Often in long grass.
Other habitats: hedgerows, cliffs.
Variable.
FLOWERS: 2.5cm (without "rays"),
5cm (with "rays"); composite with
disc florets only, but sometimes with
ray-like outer florets; bracts brown.
LEAVES: hairy; narrow, pointed;
upper unstalked, sometimes slightly
lobed, lower stalked, often slightly
toothed.

Greater Knapweed (page 37) is
similar but has flowers almost
always with "rays" and leaves
deeply lobed.

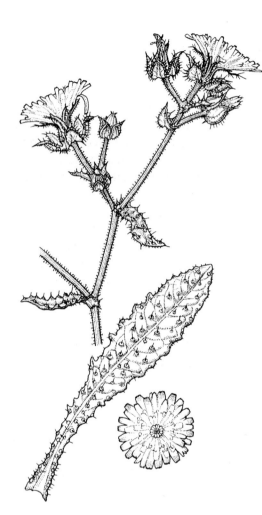

Bristly Oxtongue
(Picris echioides)
Jun – Nov   Yellow   Medium/
Tall
Other habitats: hedgerows,
shingle, cliffs.
FLOWERS: 3cm; composite with
ray florets only; bracts bristly,
outer broad, inner narrower.
Strong heady smell.
LEAVES: slightly shiny; bristly,
upper surface covered with
whitish 'pimples'; narrow,
pointed, wavy-edged; upper un-
stalked, clasping stem, lower
stalked.
STEMS: bristly.
Found almost everywhere along
the path.
Introduced.

SALT-MARSH

Salt-marsh is the first of our truly coastal habitats. It occurs on low-lying land over which sea water flows at high tide, but which is sheltered from waves. Fine particles of sand or mud are deposited and colonised by a distinctive group of plants growing between the low and high tide marks. We have also included in this habitat meadows and ditches at the upper reaches of salt water, as well as muddy shores.

Plants growing in salt-marsh are exposed to the drying effects of salt water and high winds. To enable them to survive in these conditions, they are specially adapted to ensure that that they are able to absorb and retain sufficient supplies of fresh water. Some of these adaptations are internal but others are visible; for example, many of the plants are low-growing with small, fleshy leaves.

Many salt-marshes have been destroyed by human activity such as coastal development, but those left usually retain some naturalness.

Where found on the path

Salt-marsh is a scarce habitat along the path, with small areas along the shores of the Fleet and at the Lodmoor Nature Reserve. Much larger areas are found around Poole Harbour, close to the eastern end of the path.

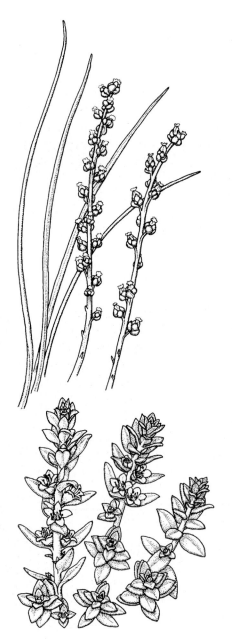

Sea Arrowgrass
(Triglochin maritimum)
Apr – Sep   Purplish green   Short/
Medium
FLOWERS: 3mm; in long narrow
spikes; no petals, 6 sepal-like parts
with whitish tuft in centre. Slightly
aromatic when rubbed.
LEAVES: fleshy; very narrow,
pointed, no ribs on back; growing
from base.
Scarce.

Sea Plantain (page 49) is similar
but has flowers with prominent
yellowish-tipped stamens and
leaves with one or more ribs on
back.

Sea-milkwort
(Glaux maritima)
May – Jul   Pale pink   Short
Creeping, mat-forming.
FLOWERS: 6mm across; nestling at
base of leaves; bell-shaped; no
petals, 5 joined petal-like sepals.
Very sweet smell.
LEAVES: slightly shiny; somewhat
fleshy; pointed; almost unstalked;
upper closely packed, lower
sparser.
A delightful small flower which
brightens up the salt-marsh; scarce.
See photograph plate 6.

Plate 1

Stinking Iris

Plate 2

Musk Thistle

Early Spider-orchid

Early Gentian

Plate 3

Dwarf Thistle

Clustered Bellflower   Bee Orchid

Plate 4

Pyramidal Orchid

Plate 5

A group of Pyramidal Orchids

Plate 6

Carline Thistle

Autumn Lady's-tresses

Sea-milkwort

Plate 7

Sea-kale

Marsh-mallow   Yellow Horned-poppy

Plate 8

Thrift in shingle habitat

Plate 9

Sea Campion

Sea Pea

Plate 10

Sea Sandwort

Sea Bindweed in shingle habitat

Plate 11

Sea-holly

Plate 12

Red Valerian

Wild Cabbage

Rock Sea-spurrey

Plate 13

Rock Sea-lavender

Plate 14

Golden-samphire

Viper's-bugloss

Ivy Broomrape

Plate 15

Sea Aster in cliff habitat

Plate 16

Rock Samphire

Greater Sea-spurrey
(Spergularia media)
May – Oct   Pinkish mauve   Short
Other habitats: rocks, cliffs.
Cushion-forming.
FLOWERS: 1.2cm; 5 petals, pinkish mauve
with white bases, sometimes almost
white all over; prominent yellow-tipped
stamens. Pleasant sweet smell. Usually
only open in bright light.
LEAVES: fleshy; narrow, pointed;
unstalked.

Lesser Sea-spurrey *(Spergularia
marina)* is similar but has smaller
flowers and petals deep pink with white
bases. See also **Rock Sea-spurrey** (page
65 and photograph plate 12).

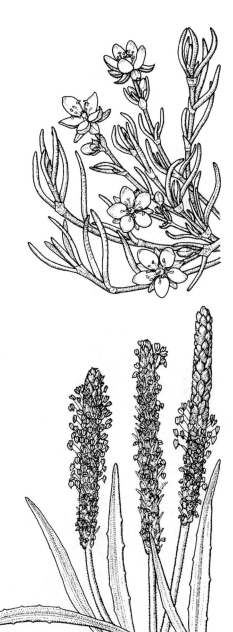

Sea Plantain
(Plantago maritima)
Jun – Sep   Purplish brown   Short/
Medium
FLOWERS: 3mm; in long narrow spikes;
4 petals, joined at base; prominent
yellowish-tipped stamens.
LEAVES: fleshy; narrow, pointed,
sometimes slightly toothed, one or more
ribs on back; growing from base.
Scarce.

Sea Arrowgrass (page 48) is similar but
has flowers without prominent stamens
and leaves with no ribs on back.

Sea-purslane
(Atriplex portulacoides)
Jun – Sep   Yellowish green   Short/ Medium
Often in dense fringes along shores and channels.
FLOWERS: 1mm (female), 2mm (male); in branched spikes; no petals; female with 2 protruding, narrow reddish parts; male cup-shaped, 5 joined sepal-like parts, prominent yellow-tipped stamens. Pungent smell.
LEAVES: pale bluish green, floury-speckled; fleshy; stalked.
STEMS: woody at base.
Scarce.

Annual Sea-blite
(Suaeda maritima)
Jun – Sep   Green   Short/Medium
Variable in habit.
Often reddening with age.
FLOWERS: 2mm; in small clusters at base of leaves; no petals, 5 sepal-like parts; yellow-tipped stamens.
LEAVES: pale bluish green, sometimes reddish; fleshy; narrow, pointed; unstalked.

Shrubby Sea-blite
(Suaeda vera)
Jun – Oct   Green   Tall
Often in dense fringes along shores and
channels.
FLOWERS: 4mm; in small clusters at base
of leaves; no petals, 5 joined sepal-like
parts; prominent yellowish-tipped
stamens.
LEAVES: bluish green, sometimes
reddish; fleshy; narrow, pointed;
closely-packed; almost unstalked.
STEMS: woody towards base.
Scarce, both along the path and
nationally.

Marsh-mallow
(Althaea officinalis)
Jul – Sep   Pale pink   Tall
Found around the upper reaches of salt
water.
FLOWERS: 3.5cm; 5 heart-shaped petals;
very pale pink with darker veins and
bases; mass of purplish-tipped stamens.
LEAVES: pale bluish green; attractively
veined; softly hairy, velvety; wavy-
edged; shallow, toothed lobes; stalked.
Beautiful and distinctive; scarce, both
along the path and nationally.
See photograph plate 7.

Sea Aster
(Aster tripolium)
Jul – Oct   Bluish mauve   Medium/
Tall
Other habitats: rocks, cliffs.
FLOWERS: 2.5cm; composite with
yellow disc florets and bluish mauve
ray florets; bracts green with purplish
edges. Pleasant sweet smell.
LEAVES: bluish green; prominent
central vein; fleshy; upper narrow,
pointed, unstalked, lower broader,
stalked.
Related to Michaelmas-daisies, which
are often found as garden escapes.
See photograph plate 15.

Glassworts
(Salicornia agg.*)*
Jul – Oct   Green   Short/Medium
A group of several very similar
species, described as one.
Often reddening with age.
FLOWERS: 1mm; usually in threes; green
base with 1-2 tiny yellow stamen-tips.
LEAVES: fleshy; scale-like; in opposite
pairs joined together around the stem.
Scarce.

Perennial Glasswort *(Sarcocornia
perennis)* is similar but patch-forming,
with creeping woody stems; rare along
the path and nationally scarce.

SHINGLE

Shingle is made up of a mass of pebbles, small stones which have been rounded by the action of the sea. The pebbles are variable in size and very fine shingle is similar to coarse sand. Shingle is also often found mixed with sand and, just as the two habitats overlap, so too do the flowers found in them. We have shown here species which are typically found in shingle.

Shingle close to the sea is unstable and easily moved by storms; further back it is more stable and this is where most flowers are found. Even in these areas the visible vegetation can sometimes be removed by very severe storms, although it often quickly recovers.

Plants growing on shingle are exposed to the drying effects of salt spray and high winds, and are specially adapted to enable them to retain fresh water. For example, many have fleshy leaves, often with a wax coating which gives them a bluish green appearance. Some also have deep roots to enable them to obtain supplies of fresh water from within the shingle.

Although some areas of shingle have been considerably affected by human activity, others, particularly parts of the Chesil Bank, retain much of their naturalness.

Where found on the path

Large areas of shingle are found where the path runs close to the Chesil Bank between Burton Bradstock and Abbotsbury and at Ferrybridge.

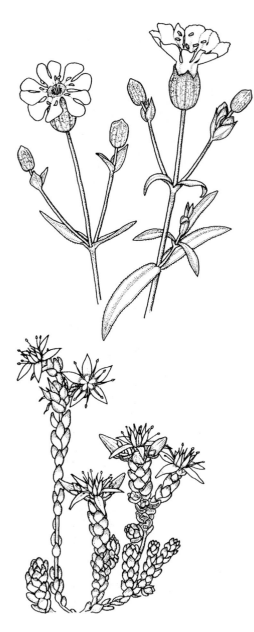

Sea Campion
(Silene uniflora)
Mar – Nov   White   Short/
Medium
Other habitats: sandy places,
cliffs.
Cushion-forming.
FLOWERS: 2.5cm; long-stalked; 5
deeply divided petals; sepal tube
swollen, light green with attractive
purplish veins. Strong sweet smell.
LEAVES: bluish green, waxy;
slightly fleshy; narrow, pointed;
mostly unstalked.
Found in profusion in places along
the path.
See photograph plate 9.

Biting Stonecrop
(Sedum acre)
May – Jul   Bright yellow   Short
Other habitats: rocks, cliffs, walls.
Mat-forming.
FLOWERS: 1.5cm; in small clusters;
star-shaped; 5 well-separated
pointed petals; prominent yellow
stamens.
LEAVES: yellowish green, often
reddish-tinged; fleshy; very small,
closely-packed, unstalked.

White Stonecrop *(Sedum album)*,
found on cliffs, has smaller white
or pinkish flowers in large
clusters.
Introduced.

Sea-kale
(Crambe maritima)
May – Jul   White   Medium/Tall
Other habitats: sandy places, cliffs.
Often in large clumps.
Squat.
FLOWERS: 1.5cm; in large clusters;
4 rounded petals in cross shape;
prominent yellow stamens.
Pleasant sweet smell.
LEAVES: pale bluish green; fleshy;
wavy-edged; variable in shape;
upper clasping stem, lower long-
stalked.
Very common in places along the
path.
See photograph plate 7.

Sea Pea
(Lathyrus japonicus)
May-Sep   Purple   Short
Often in large patches.
FLOWERS: 2cm long; pea-type; in
long-stalked heads; purple turning
bluish, paler centre. Pleasant
unusual sweetish smell.
FRUIT: pea-like pods.
LEAVES: bluish green; attractively
veined; slightly fleshy; each with
about 4-5 pairs of leaflets and
usually a tendril at the end.
The roots go deep into the shingle;
rare along the path and nationally
scarce.
See photograph plate 9.

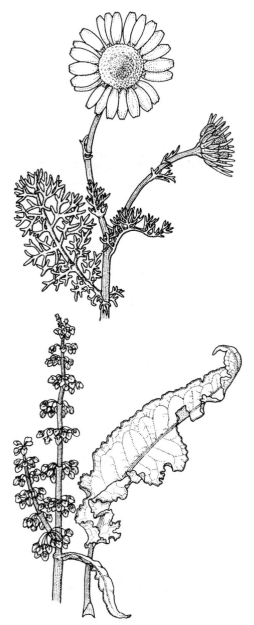

Sea Mayweed
(Tripleurospermum maritimum)
May – Nov   White   Short/Medium
Other habitats: sandy places, cliffs.
FLOWERS: 4cm; composite with
yellow disc florets and white ray
florets – like large daisies.
LEAVES: deeply divided, branching
several times into fleshy segments.

Scentless Mayweed *(Tripleuro-spermum inodorum)*, often found in
cultivated ground, is similar but has
leaves with narrower, non-fleshy,
feathery segments. Introduced.
Hybrids, with leaves in-between the
two, are often found.
Oxeye Daisy (page 29) has similar
flowers to both but leaves toothed or
lobed.

Curled Dock
(Rumex crispus)
Jun – Oct   Green   Tall
Other habitats: hedgerows, dry
grassland, sandy places.
FLOWERS: 4mm; in whorls on long,
branched spikes; 6 sepal-like parts,
often turning red.
LEAVES: mid-green turning reddish;
rather leathery; narrow, pointed,
very wavy-edged.
STEMS: often reddish, rather woody.
The dead stems remain over the
winter.

Yellow Horned-poppy
(Glaucium flavum)
Jun – Oct   Yellow   Medium/Tall
Other habitats: sandy places, cliffs.
FLOWERS: 6cm; 4 delicate, silky petals;
prominent mass of orange stamens.
FRUIT: long, narrow, curved pods – the
"horns".
LEAVES: pale bluish green; slightly fleshy;
very hairy; wavy-edged; toothed lobes;
upper unstalked, clasping stem, lower
stalked, in rosette at base.
Very attractive and conspicuous.
See photograph plate 7.

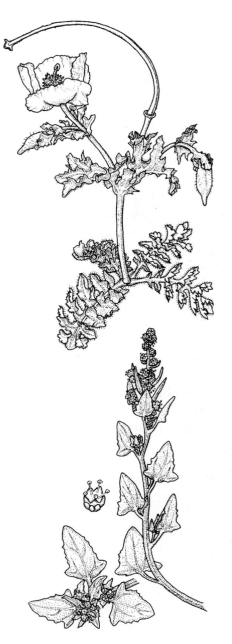

Babington's Orache
(Atriplex glabriuscula)
Jul – Aug   Green   Short/Medium
Often at the drift line on beaches.
Other habitat: muddy shores.
Usually sprawling.
FLOWERS: 2mm (male); in leafy spikes; no
petals; female obscure, male cup-shaped
with 5 joined sepal-like parts, edges
often reddish.
LEAVES: bluish green, floury-speckled;
prominently veined; fairly fleshy;
triangular with winged bases, slightly
toothed; stalked.

Spear-leaved Orache *(Atriplex
prostrata)*, often found inland, is very
similar but has leaves less floury-
speckled. Variable: the two are often
difficult to distinguish.

SANDY PLACES

This habitat includes places such as sandy beaches, sand dunes, sandy grassland and sandy shingle. As described on page 53, the flowers found in sand and shingle overlap; we have shown here species which are typically found in sand.

Sand close to the sea is unstable and easily moved by high winds, but many plants found here can survive being buried by growing up through the covering sand. Plants themselves assist in the formation of dunes by binding the sand and old-established dunes can become quite stable.

As with flowers found in other coastal habitats, those in sandy places are adapted to overcome the drying effects of salt spray and high winds, and the shortage of fresh water. As a result, many are short with fleshy leaves and have roots which grow deep into the sand.

Many sandy places, especially at seaside resorts, have been substantially altered by development. Where human pressure has been less intense, some naturalness remains.

Where found on the path

The largest area of partly natural sandy places is at Studland Bay, where there are extensive sandy beaches and dunes. Smaller areas are found near Burton Bradstock and at Ferrybridge.

Common Stork's-bill
(Erodium cicutarium)
Mar – Oct   Purplish pink   Short
Other habitat: cliffs.
Often in bare places or short turf.
Variable.
FLOWERS: 1cm; 5 petals, soon lost;
sometimes white.
FRUIT: with narrow, pointed "stork's
bill".
LEAVES: hairy; divided into leaflets with
toothed lobes; often only in rosette at
base.

Sea Stork's-bill *(Erodium maritimum)*,
found on cliffs, has much smaller
flowers, usually without petals, and
undivided leaves with toothed lobes;
scarce.

Sea Sandwort
(Honckenya peploides)
Apr – Jul   White   Short
Other habitat: shingle.
Creeping, often in large carpeting
patches.
FLOWERS: 6mm (female), 1cm (male),
usually on separate plants; usually 5
well-separated petals; prominent
stamens on male flowers. Pleasant
sweet smell.
LEAVES: yellowish green with
translucent edges; shiny; fleshy;
pointed oval; unstalked.
Scarce.
See photograph plate 10.

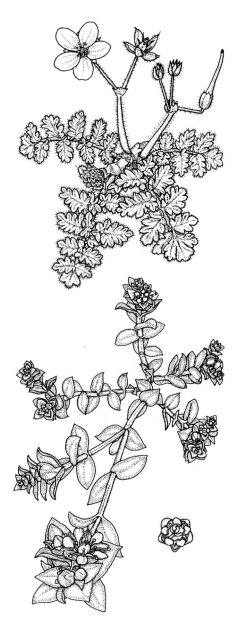

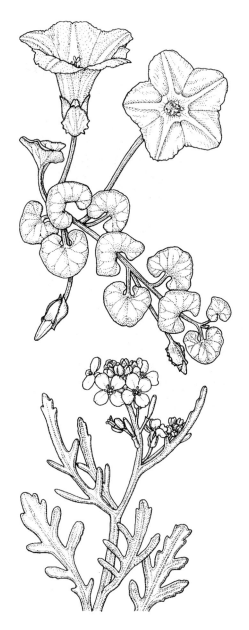

Sea Bindweed
(Calystegia soldanella)
Jun – Aug   Pink and white   Short
Other habitat: shingle.
Creeping, patch-forming.
FLOWERS: 6cm; trumpet-shaped; 5
petal lobes, joined nearly to top,
pale pink with white stripes.
LEAVES: dark green; fairly shiny;
attractively veined; fleshy; kidney-
shaped, slightly cupped; long-
stalked.
Scarce and very attractive.
See photograph plate 10.

Sea Rocket
(Cakile maritima)
Jun – Oct   Lilac to white   Short/
Medium
Other habitat: shingle.
Usually at the drift line on beaches.
Often sprawling.
FLOWERS: 1.5cm; in short spikes; 4
slightly notched petals, in cross
shape. Pleasant sweet smell.
LEAVES: bluish green; slightly shiny;
fleshy; usually with irregular lobes
but sometimes very narrow and
unlobed.

Sea-holly
(Eryngium maritimum)
Jul – Sep   Pale blue   Short/
Medium
Other habitat: shingle.
FLOWERS: 3mm; in tight,
hemispherical, spiny heads;
prominent white-tipped stamens.
Pleasant sweetish smell.
LEAVES: very pale bluish green;
attractive whitish veins and
edges; holly-like; upper
unstalked, each usually with 3-5
leaflets in whorl around stem;
lower roundish, deeply lobed,
long-stalked, growing from
base.
A beautiful and memorable
plant; rare.
See photograph plate 11.

ROCKS AND CLIFFS

Cliff tops often merge into dry grassland and the flowers found in the two habitats overlap. Similarly, flowers found lower down on cliffs and on rocks close to the sea overlap with those found in other coastal habitats. We have shown here species which are typically found on rocks and cliffs. We have also included in this habitat undercliffs, areas of often terraced, lower cliffs resulting from landfalls, which sometimes support uncommon species.

Plants growing on seaside rocks and low down on cliffs have to overcome the drying effects of salt spray and high winds, and there is little soil to provide fresh water. As a result, the flowers here have adaptations found in other coastal species, such as fleshy leaves and deep roots.

The underlying geology of a cliff greatly influences the flowers which grow there; for example, many of the species found on chalk cliffs are different from those on less calcareous ones (see 'Soils' page 14).

Besides coastal rocks and cliffs, we have included in this section two man-made habitats which share some of their features, old quarries and walls.

Of the habitats in this book, rocks and cliffs are the least affected by human activity, due to their inaccessibility, and many retain much of their naturalness.

Where found on the path

Rocks and cliffs with a good variety of flowers are found around Durdle Door and Lulworth Cove, on Portland and in many parts of Purbeck.

Danish Scurvygrass
(Cochlearia danica)
Feb – Sep   Pinkish mauve to
white   Short
Other habitats: shingle, sandy
places.
Variable.
FLOWERS: 5mm; in clusters; 4
petals, in cross shape; prominent
yellow-tipped stamens. Pleasant
smell.
LEAVES: slightly shiny; fleshy;
stalked; upper ivy-shaped; lower
more or less heart-shaped,
growing from base.

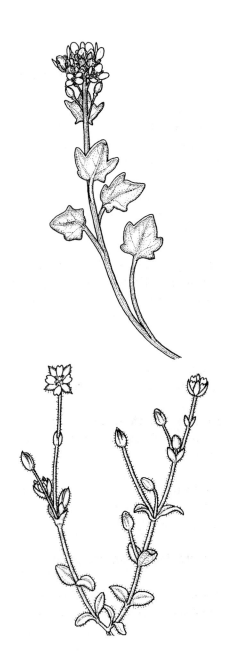

Sea Mouse-ear
(Cerastium diffusum)
Mar – Jun   White   Short
Other habitats: shingle, sandy
places.
FLOWERS: 5mm; in small loose
clusters; usually 4, sometimes 5,
slightly notched petals; sepals
slightly longer than petals.
LEAVES: darkish green; stickily
hairy; pointed oval; unstalked.
STEMS: stickily hairy.

One of several similar – and
easily confused – Mouse-ears
found along the path.

Thrift, Sea Pink
(Armeria maritima)
Mar – Nov   Pink   Short/Medium
Other habitats: salt-marsh, shingle,
sandy places.
Cushion-forming.
FLOWERS: 1cm; in hemispherical
heads on long, hairy stalks; 5
petals, joined at the very base;
pale to deep pink, sometimes
white. Pleasant sweet smell.
LEAVES: bluish green; central vein;
slightly hairy; very narrow,
pointed; growing from base.
For many of us the flower most
evocative of the seaside.
See photograph plate 8.

Wild Cabbage, Sea Cabbage
(Brassica oleracea var. oleracea)
Apr – Jul   Yellow   Tall
Usually on calcareous cliffs.
FLOWERS: 2.5cm; in long, branched
spikes; 4 petals in cross shape.
LEAVES: bluish green, waxy;
prominent veins; fleshy; wavy-
edged; upper unstalked, clasping
stem, lower stalked.
STEMS: woody and leaf-scarred at
base.
Closely related to cultivated
cabbages; nationally scarce.
See photograph plate 12.

Portland Spurge
(Euphorbia portlandica)
Apr – Oct   Yellow   Short/Medium
Usually on calcareous cliffs.
Other habitats: shingle, sandy places.
Often reddening with age.
FLOWERS: 2mm (female), tiny (male);
in umbrella-shaped clusters; no petals
or sepals; one female with several
male flowers and 4 yellow crescent-
shaped parts inside a leafy cup.
LEAVES: bluish green; oval with
pointed tip and tapered base;
prominent central rib below;
unstalked.
STEMS: often woody at base.
Several other Spurges are also found
along the path.

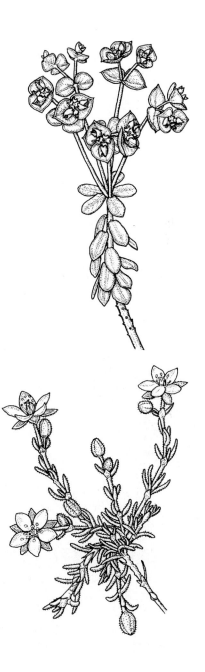

Rock Sea-spurrey
(Spergularia rupicola)
Apr – Oct   Pink   Short
Sometimes on walls.
Cushion-forming.
FLOWERS: 1cm; in small clusters; 5
petals; prominent yellow-tipped
stamens. Pleasant sweet smell.
Usually only open in bright light.
LEAVES: greyish green; fleshy; stickily
hairy; narrow, pointed; unstalked.
STEMS: stickily hairy.
See photograph plate 12 and **Greater
Sea-spurrey** (page 49).

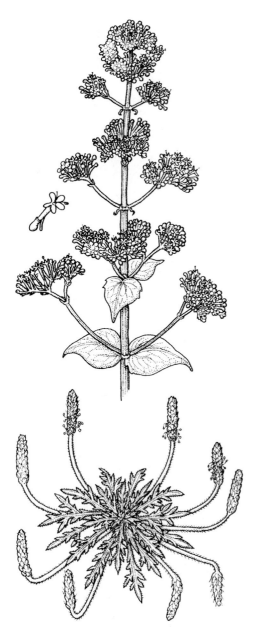

Red Valerian
(Centranthus ruber)
Apr – Oct   Red to pink   Medium/
Tall
Often in old quarries or on walls.
Other habitats: dry grassland,
shingle.
Clump-forming.
FLOWERS: 6mm across; in branched
spikes; tubular with 5 irregular petal
lobes, spur at base; sometimes
white. Strong sweet smell.
LEAVES: bluish green; slightly
fleshy; pointed; upper broad,
unstalked, clasping stem, lower
narrow, stalked.
Introduced; a naturalised garden
plant.
See photograph plate 12.

Buck's-horn Plantain
(Plantago coronopus)
Apr – Oct   Light brown   Short
Other habitats: waste ground,
shingle, sandy places.
Often in bare places.
Variable in size; sometimes tiny.
FLOWERS: 3mm; in spikes on downy
stalks; 4 petals, joined at base; long
yellowish-tipped stamens.
LEAVES: greyish green; very hairy;
narrow, pointed; lobed and/or
toothed – variable; in rosette at
base.

Ivy-leaved Toadflax
(Cymbalaria muralis)
Apr – Nov   Pale mauve   Short
Often on walls.
Other habitat: shingle.
Trailing or creeping with long,
often reddish, rooting stems.
FLOWERS: 1cm across; long-stalked;
2-lipped; pale mauve with darker
veins; lower lip 3-lobed with 2
orange eyes; short spur behind.
LEAVES: often purplish-tinged;
slightly shiny; ivy-shaped; long-
stalked.
Introduced; a naturalised garden
plant.

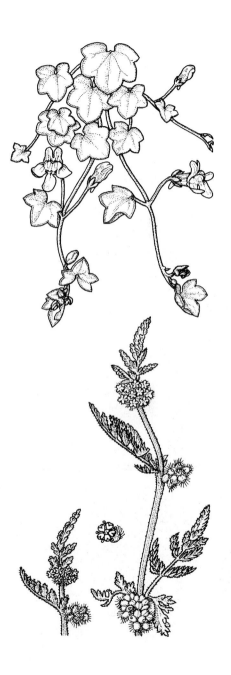

Knotted Hedge-parsley
(Torilis nodosa)
May – Jul   White or pale pink
Short/Medium
Usually on cliff tops.
Slender.
FLOWERS: 2mm; in small, tight
umbrella-shaped clusters, each
opposite a leaf; 5 petals; prominent
stamens.
FRUIT: sticky burs.
LEAVES: hairy; delicate, fern-like,
divided into leaflets with toothed
lobes.
Attractive but easily overlooked.

Nottingham Catchfly
(Silene nutans)
May – Jul   Creamy white   Medium
Usually on chalk cliffs.
FLOWERS: 2cm; in small drooping
clusters; 5 deeply-divided, narrow
petals; prominent greenish-tipped
stamens. Opening fully, with petals
rolled back and strong sweet smell, in
the evening.
LEAVES: light green; softly hairy; edges
wavy and turned inwards; upper
narrow, pointed, unstalked, clasping
stem; lower broader, stalked, at base.
Scarce, both along the path and
nationally.

White Campion *(Silene latifolia)*,
often found on verges, is similar but
has larger, pure white flowers with
less divided, broader petals.
Introduced.

Slender Thistle
(Carduus tenuiflorus)
May – Aug   Purplish pink   Short/
Medium/Tall
Other habitat: verges.
FLOWERS: 1cm; in small clusters;
composite with disc florets only,
purplish pink turning mauvish; bracts
purplish.
LEAVES: light green; cottony-haired,
especially below; narrow, pointed,
wavy-edged; deeply lobed, sharp
whitish spines on tips.
STEMS: cottony-haired, spiny-winged.

Viper's-bugloss
(Echium vulgare)
May – Oct   Bright blue   Medium/Tall
Other habitat: dry grassland.
FLOWERS: 1.5cm across; in leafy spikes; more
or less bell-shaped with 5 unequal petal
lobes; pink buds; long protruding stamens
with purple bases and whitish tips.
LEAVES: greyish green; prominent central
vein; very hairy; narrow, pointed; upper
unstalked, lower stalked, in rosette at base.
STEMS: roughly hairy.
See photograph plate 14.

Common Centaury
(Centaurium erythraea)
May – Oct   Pink   Short/Medium
Other habitats: dry grassland, sandy places.
FLOWERS: 1.2cm; usually 5 broad petals,
joined at base; prominent yellow-tipped
stamens. Often only fully open in sunshine.
LEAVES: yellowish green; slightly shiny;
unstalked; upper in opposite pairs, lower in
rosette at base.

Lesser Centaury *(Centaurium pulchellum)*
has smaller, deep pink flowers with 4-5
narrower petals. Often tiny.

Slender Centaury *(Centaurium*
tenuiflorum), found on undercliffs, usually
has white flowers; its only sites in Britain
are along the coast between Charmouth and
West Bay.

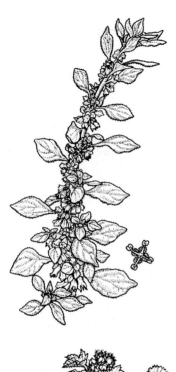

Pellitory-of-the-wall

(Parietaria judaica)

May – Oct   Greenish red   Short/
Medium

Often on walls but also found on
rocks and cliffs.

Other habitat: shingle.

FLOWERS: 2mm (female), 4mm
(male); in clusters at leaf junctions;
no petals, 4 sepal-like parts, joined
at base; male with prominent
whitish-tipped stamens.

LEAVES: light to mid-green;
attractively veined; softly hairy;
pointed; stalked.

STEMS: reddish.

Common Mallow

(Malva sylvestris)

May – Oct   Pinkish purple   Short/
Medium/Tall

Other habitats: verges, shingle.
Variable in habit: sprawling to
erect.

FLOWERS: 4cm; 5 well-separated,
heart-shaped petals, pinkish purple
with darker veins; prominent mass
of white-tipped stamens. Pleasant
sweet smell.

LEAVES: prominent, often reddish,
veins; softly hairy; wavy-edged,
rather wrinkled; roundish with
shallow, toothed lobes; long-
stalked.

Introduced.

See **Tree-mallow** (page 21).

Wild Carrot
(Daucus carota ssp. *carota)*
May – Nov   White   Medium/Tall
Other habitat: dry grassland.
FLOWERS: 5mm; in umbrella-shaped
clusters; 5 irregularly-shaped petals,
often pinkish-tinged; flowers in centre
of cluster sometimes purplish.
Pleasant sweetish smell.
LEAVES: hairy; delicate, fern-like;
divided into leaflets with toothed
lobes; base sheathing stem.

Sea Carrot *(Daucus carota* ssp.
gummifer), found very close to the
sea, is similar but has fleshy, less
divided leaves. Plants with leaves in-
between the two are often found.

Weld
(Reseda luteola)
Jun – Sep   Greenish yellow   Tall
Usually on calcareous cliffs.
FLOWERS: 4mm; in long narrow spikes;
4 petals, the upper 3 lobed, the lowest
one unlobed; prominent mass of
yellow-tipped stamens. Strongish
smell.
LEAVES: fairly shiny; prominent central
vein; very narrow, pointed, wavy-
edged; unstalked.
Striking and attractive.
Introduced.

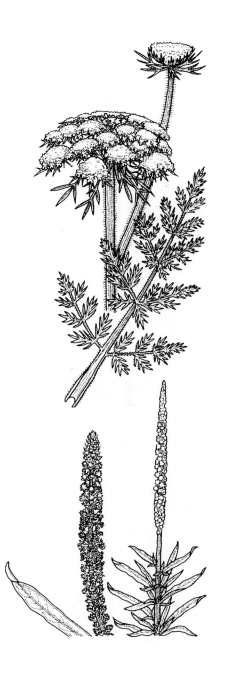

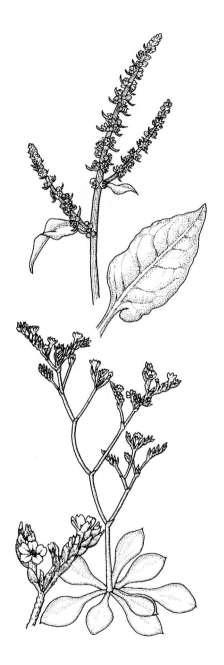

Sea Beet
(Beta vulgaris ssp. *maritima)*
Jun – Oct   Yellowish green
Medium/Tall
Other habitats: muddy shores, shingle,
sandy places.
Sprawling.
Often reddish-tinged.
FLOWERS: 5mm; in branched spikes; no
petals, 5 sepal-like parts, joined at
base. Pleasant sweet smell.
LEAVES: shiny; prominent central vein;
leathery; wavy-edged; upper
unstalked, lower stalked.
Closely related to cultivated beets.

Rock Sea-lavenders
(Limonium binervosum agg.*)*
Jul – Oct   Mauvish purple   Short/
Medium
On calcareous rocks and cliffs.
Other habitat: salt-marsh.
A group of several similar species,
described as one; the illustration and
photograph show *Limonium
dodartiforme.*
FLOWERS: 6mm; in branched spikes; 5
heart-shaped, overlapping petals,
joined at base.
LEAVES: bluish green; pointed tip; in
rosettes at base.
Elegant and attractive.
See photograph plate 13.

Golden-samphire
(Inula crithmoides)
Jul – Oct   Yellow   Short/Medium/
Tall
On calcareous rocks and cliffs.
FLOWERS: 2.5cm; composite with
golden yellow disc florets and short
yellow ray florets; bracts light
green, fleshy.
LEAVES: fleshy; very narrow, often
with 3-pointed tip; unstalked,
densely packed around stem.
Strongly and distinctively aromatic
when crushed.
Nationally scarce.
See photograph plate 14.

Rock Samphire
(Crithmum maritimum)
Jul – Oct   Greenish yellow   Short/
Medium/Tall
Other habitat: shingle.
FLOWERS: 3mm; in umbrella-shaped
clusters; 5 petals, curled over
towards centre; buds often pinkish;
prominent pale yellow-tipped
stamens. Aromatic.
LEAVES: bluish green; fleshy; deeply
divided, repeatedly branching 3
ways into narrow, pointed
segments. Aromatic when crushed.
See photograph plate 16.

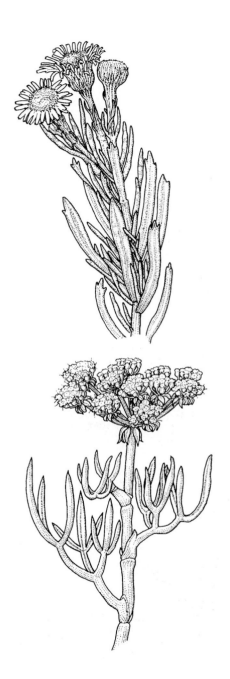

BIBLIOGRAPHY

ALLAN, B., WOODS, P. (1993) *Wild Orchids of Scotland.* HMSO. Reprinted (1993).

ALLEN, D.J. (2000) *Wild Flowers of the East Devon Coast.* Quantock Nature.

BARRETT, J.H., NIMMO, M. (1986) *Identifying flowers common along the Coast Path.* Pembrokeshire Coast National Park Authority. Reprinted (1988).

BLAMEY, M., FITTER, R. (1979) *Collins Handguide to the Wild Flowers of Britain and Northern Europe.* William Collins Sons & Co. Ltd.

BLAMEY, M., GREY-WILSON, C. (1989) *The Illustrated Flora of Britain and Northern Europe.* Hodder and Stoughton.

BOWEN, H.J.M. (2000) *The Flora of Dorset.* Pisces Publications.

CLAPHAM, A.R., TUTIN, T.G., WARBURG, E.F. (1959) *Excursion Flora of the British Isles.* Cambridge University Press. 3rd Ed. (1981). Reprinted (1995).

CRAMB, P. & M. (2000) *Wild Flowers of Perthshire.* P. & M. Cramb.

DORSET WILDLIFE TRUST (1997) *The Natural History of Dorset.* The Dovecote Press Ltd.

FITTER, R., FITTER, A., BLAMEY, M. (1974) *Collins Pocket Guide The Wild Flowers of Britain and Northern Europe.* HarperCollins. 5th Ed. (1996).

GIBBONS, B. (2000) *Wild Flowers* (Tracker Guide). Chancellor Press.

GILMOUR, J., WALTERS, M. (1954) *Wild Flowers* (New Naturalist No. 5). Collins.

HEPBURN, I. (1952) *Flowers of the Coast* (New Naturalist No. 24). Collins. Reprinted (1966).

HORSFALL, A. (1991) *Names of Wild Flowers in Dorset.* A. Horsfall.

GOOD, R.D. (1948) *A Geographical Handbook of the Dorset Flora.* Dorset Natural History and Archaeological Society.

JENKINSON, M.N. (1991) *Wild Orchids of Dorset.* Orchid Sundries Ltd.

KEBLE MARTIN, W. (1965) *The Concise British Flora in Colour.* Ebury Press and Michael Joseph.

MABEY, R. (1996) *Flora Britannica.* Sinclair-Stevenson.

MAHON, A., PEARMAN, D.A., Eds. (1993) *Endangered Wildlife in Dorset.* Dorset Environmental Records Centre.

MANSEL-PLEYDELL, J.C. (1874) *The Flora of Dorsetshire.* Privately printed. 2nd Ed. (1895).

MARREN, P. (1999) *Britain's Rare Flowers.* T. & A.D. Poyser Ltd.

PETRY, L.C., NORMAN, M.G. (1963) *A Beachcomber's Botany.* The Chatham Conservation Foundation, Inc. Reprinted (1982).

PHILLIPS, R. (1977) *Wild Flowers of Britain.* Pan Books Ltd.

PRESTON, C.D., PEARMAN, D.A., DINES, T.D., Eds. (2002) *New Atlas of the British & Irish Flora.* Oxford University Press.

READER'S DIGEST (1981) *Field Guide to the Wild Flowers of Britain.* The Reader's Digest Association Limited. Reprinted (1989).

RICH, T.C.G., JERMY, A.C. (1998) *Plant Crib 1998.* Botanical Society of the British Isles.

ROBERTS, S. (1984) *The Wild Flowers of Dorset.* The Dovecote Press Ltd. Reprinted (1989).

ROSE, F. (1981) *The Wild Flower Key.* Frederick Warne. Reissued (1991).

STACE, C. (1991) *New Flora of the British Isles.* Cambridge University Press. 2nd Ed. (1997).

STEWART, A., PEARMAN, D.A., PRESTON, C.D., Eds. (1994) *Scarce Plants in Britain.* JNCC.

TARR, R. (1989) *National Trail Guide 11, South West Coast Path, Exmouth to Poole.* Aurum Press Ltd. in association with the Countryside Commission and the Ordnance Survey. Revised Ed. (2002).

TOMLINSON, N., Ed. (1997) *The Flowering Plants of Chesil Beach at Portland.* Chesil Bank and the Fleet Nature Reserve.

WIGGINTON, M.J., Ed. (1999) *British Red Data Books. 1 Vascular Plants.* Joint Nature Conservation Committee. 3rd Ed.

INDEX